REFLECTIONS
of Nature

Poetry by Gerard Traub

Images by Nelus Oana

Front cover: "Fire and Flowers" by Nelus Oana. Oil painting on composition board 120 x 90 cms. All paintings featured throughout this publication are Copyright © 2020 Nelus Oana

All poetry Copyright © 2020 Gerard Traub

All rights reserved. Content in this book is protected by copyright and all intellectual property belongs to the author. This book and its contents may not be sold, used, published, reproduced, distributed or copied without the author's express permission. All enquiries should be made to the author.

National Library of Australia C.I.P data:
Gerard Traub/Poetry

First published in Australia in 2020 by MMH Press
www.mmhpress.com

978-0-6488203-7-6 (e)
978-0-6488203-8-3 (sc)
978-0-6488203-9-0 (hc)

Acknowledgements

In loving memory of my mother Beryl whose garden was always in bloom.

Thank you to my wife Glenda and daughter Alicia, all of my family, Nelus for his beautiful paintings, his wife Andra, Karen at MMH Press, Jennifer at Clarke Street Creative and everyone who made this book possible.

I acknowledge all of the Traditional Custodians of Australia's ancient and sacred land.

This book is dedicated to all those who dare to dream a world of new horizons and a greater humanity to come.

Introduction

Reflections of Nature is written through a life filter that we all would benefit from embracing in our lifetime. There is wisdom woven through the inner poetic language that will play a melodic dance with your thoughts, leaving you mesmerised and wanting more. The harmony between Gerard's words and Nelus' images is genius in action.

This book is a gift to the world.

Karen McDermott

Contents

Foreword	09
The Forest	11
Dance of Air	12
Where Stars Awaken	13
Beckoning Tides	15
Moments of the Miraculous	16
No Skies Compare	18
A Timeless Journey	19
Morning	21
Alight in Fire	22
Worlds Within	24
Noosa	25
Spring	27
An Endless Ocean	28
Pandanus	30
Horizons	31
Melody of Light	33
The Dawning	34
Pomona Sunset	36
The Valour of Seasons	37
Silhouette	39

Surrender	40
The Poetry	42
You Are	43
Reign of Fire	45
An Endless Bough	46
A Song of Birds	48
Tanawha	49
Communion	51
Stillness	52
Every World Akin	54
Reflections	55
Night	57
Upon a Butterfly's Dream	58
Shores to Seasons	60
Inside Every Heart	61
Across Winter Skies	63
Sentinel	64
Peregian Beach	66
The Spark	67
I am Flower	69
Beyond the Eye	70
Mooloolaba Summer	72
Point Pure	73

The Unseen	75
Song for the Earth	76
All Elements Convene	78
We are the Song	79
One Seed	81
Breathe the Silence	82
Poised	83

Foreword

We invite the reader to open the pages of this book with a quiet mind and heart. Reflect upon the words and colourful images inspired by the beauty of the Sunshine Coast, Queensland, the vast Australian landscape and all of the natural world that not only surrounds us, but breathes every moment with us. Consider each page like a thread weaving into the next to form an intricate tapestry.

In silence, there is also a poetry waiting to be discovered behind the word and beyond the page.

The Forest

The forest sees you
every trunk and limb
it listens to your breath
each footstep taken
upon its ancient ground.

The forest seeks communion
with your inner knowing
even the birds can sense your song
the wings you long to find
the heart that veils
your blood of lifetimes.
Born of soul and spark
extinguished then reclaimed again
from embers unseen to the eye.

The forest beckons for your return
to stand centred
to aspire to the light
here and beyond any canopy.
How majestic in stature
embracing a love for all seasons
content in storm and blaze of sun.

Let the forest see you
as it reveals its timeless fire
where every seed finds promise.

In your stillness it may even speak.

Dance of Air

Feeling a breath of wind
the rush of sun
flooding every leaf
and stretch of trees.

The morning almost
seized by sound
crowding my senses
before a bird
hovers silent in flight
above the moment
content in this dance of air.

Where Stars Awaken

Where stars awaken
like seeds aflame
where waters reflect
a myriad of suns
where earth weaves
into tides beyond
and worlds within
to without are one.

Where every moment
whispers to the soul
where heart soars
upon boundless wings
where words arise
from a silent breath
and the finite
flowers into everything.

Beckoning Tides

From beckoning tides
to every shore
the ocean finds its song
from whispers of fields
to the crying forests
such bitter seeds sown too long.

How common these shadows
casting worlds into night
the air closing winter's cold
beyond any earth laid bare
the mountain forever stands
no more to be silenced and sold.

I hear the echoes
drumming a new day
with voices gathering upon the wind
where dreams take flight
and hearts bear courage
horizons awakening to another spring.

Moments of the Miraculous

Moments of the miraculous
behind every flower unfolding
inside each colour and luminous form
beyond the charge of atoms
endless skies to fathomless oceans
awakening realms between stillness and storm.

No Skies Compare

To live as a flower
unfolding to the autumn sun
rising with scent of endless forest
each dawn until another day is done.

To flow as the tide
surrenders to a greater hand
as oceans embrace light and shore
breathing every stretch of sand.

To awaken as a bird in flight
finding wings in silent prayer
with faith from seed toward soaring oak
such moments where no skies compare.

A Timeless Journey

Upon a timeless journey our hearts prevail
free to walk the wind and breathe the stars
now taking flight in an endless dance
eternity unfolding across worlds afar.

Awakened to light surrender
of dawns and aeons entwined
from circle to ascent complete
braving every shadow to shine.

Beyond the skies and distant shores
across the infinite seas we sail
finding soul when tide and truth returns
upon a timeless journey our hearts prevail.

Morning

Where rising sun
floods skies of radiant blue
another night retreating
with whispers of morning dew.

Every branch drawing breath
stretching to courageous height
hidden fire behind each flower
beyond any bird in flight.

Alight in Fire

We are ancient embers glowing
hearts alight in fire
emerging from the shadows
born of sun and soul desire.

We are worlds weaving and unfolding
dreams hidden to the eye
a palette of many colours
beyond any shore or sky.

We are purest waters flowing
veiled in a circle of tides
endless breath from blood to being
ascent by dance and stride.

We are countless atoms colliding
configurations come every flame
to embrace both tempest and calm
all becoming until soul reclaimed.

Worlds Within

Worlds within a sea shell
veils upon infinity
mountains countless
behind pebble and sand
forests to tower
from the smallest seed.

Unfolding into moments
with vision far clearer
beyond the eyes
a drop holding oceans
and more to come
stars from first breath to dying
coursing through our veins.

Galaxies between atoms
suns against a candle flame
how many stories beneath
one word and line
dreams from every bird of feather?

Noosa

Gulls sweeping wing
across lapping waves
cloud that veils
the winter sun
from stretch of sand
to horizons beyond
where moments and eternity
fold into one.

Spring

Between hours languishing
and the fleeting of spring
my eyes dance amongst the leaves
quivering upon such restless air
as clouds drift silent and beyond.

Under a breath of shade
while the sun strikes down
from surrounding birdsong
to the heave of distant waves
all swarming to find my senses.

An Endless Ocean

The sky an endless ocean
beyond every tide and fathom
drowning me inside your vastness.

I surrender between here and horizons
where beauty with my own becoming
breathes moments into silence.

Pandanus

A myriad of fronds
flame-like and tangled green
leaping into this salted wind
here under an endless sky
across terrain of stretching sands
where sea casts a turquoise expanse
come horizons and distant sails
summoned all to the eye.

Horizons

Across heaving oceans
and towering mountains
waves that glisten to the eye
from forest to field
come awaken with heart
wider than horizons of sky.

Worlds within a flower
calling in whisper
seed to tallest trunk entwined
under blazing sun
or drenching rain
this breath of nature beyond our designs.

Melody of Light

In surrounds of green
I surrender here
with every chorus of colour
crowding the eye.

Upon silent reflections
awakening breath to song
drenched and dappled
in a melody of light.

The Dawning

If I could rise
into the sky
clothe myself
in endless cloud
as the sun awakens
upon my own dawning
finding quiet wings
and colours aloud.

If I could merge
with every ocean
lose myself
in depths of blue
to inhabit the tides
each ebb and flow
until reaching shores
of golden hues.

If I could curl
into a fire
feel myself
in leaps of flame
from the darkest night
to summer's first breath
seeking a boundless heart
where worlds untamed.

If I could summon
the forests and fields
reclaim myself
as a seed dreams to flower
witnessing all the earth
between delight and dread
stretching across horizons
here until my final hour.

Pomona Sunset

As sunlight fades
from the shimmering leaves
and each heaving trunk
sighs to evening's surrender
another day's sojourn
seasoned with every hour
where time follows close
between cold and tender.

When restless air
breathes calm to the eye
and skies close sudden
into a winter's grey
each flower holds faith
through darkest night
until dawn and birdsong
find delight in play.

The Valour of Seasons

Through the valour of seasons
falling snow to blazing sun
where touch of skin
meets the heart's embrace
dancing light and shadows as one.

With rise of silent breath
only a whisper to the wind
as every ocean calls wide
weaving a forest of memories
first light to another season's end.

Silhouette

Moonlight dappled
through ascending boughs
leaves transforming into silhouette
behind this veil of night
with horizons losing sight
until another dawn and heart content.

Branches clawing blind
wrestling with the wind
swept into a sudden fray
if all to steal an hour
and each star a budding flower
many to pluck rather than gaze.

Surrender

Upon oceans adrift
sands swept across
infinite shores and time
into the endless blue
I surrender all
under boundless skies.

Where hearts calling
to horizons beyond
closer to turning tides
upon oceans adrift
waiting for the hour
until every storm subsides.

The Poetry

Where wind plays
with leaf and flower
forests whisper
in silent word
when horizons call
from a distant dream
come find the music
beyond all you have heard.

Can you hear the poetry?

Where wings soar
upon golden skies
steepest mountains descend
into fields of green
when sea meets shore
a million suns glisten
come awaken your eyes
beyond all you have seen.

Can you see the poetry?

You Are

You are
wind and water
fire of the sun
you are mountain
to endless forest
the myriad woven as one.

You are
the breath of tides
oceans to every shore
you are being
where infinite stars reside
of flesh and far more.

You are
seed of earth
fruit before the flower
you are sung from silence
precious light aflame
forever timeless to the hour.

Reign of Fire

Fire from spark awakening
how leaping tongues of flame entrance
belly swelled voracious fed
unbridled rage or primordial dance?

Crackles swirling upward storm
consuming all a fearsome path
with reign of beast every swarm ablaze
until fall of ash and cinder epitaph.

An Endless Bough

A flame behind the sky
sounds still lingering
beneath the silence
where colours find no palette
and landscapes find less form
with the shadows of night unveiling
the stars return to scale our skies
watching horizons echo the sun's descent.

Let this day to every hour
awaken and swarm our hearts
these eyes saving few tears
shed in the ashes of delight
to breathe as a slumbering brook
feel every swirling and stone's caress.

Born into the skin of a thousand lifetimes
when the wilderness remained untamed
drawn to where the circles danced
once leaping beyond any languish of seasons
until now a mere leaf
common before an endless bough.

A Song of Birds

Circling in flight
sinking into the sky
where darkness breathes
above the world
and no wings collide.

As the sun surrenders
to another day
distant birds dissolve
until only the light
inside us remains.

Tanawha

Sun dappled upon leaf
stretching light
through trunk and canopy
where trees rising
to embrace an endless sky
from many a palette green.

Behind a murmur of wind
a quiet symphony plays
as I breathe the fragrant air
heard not with ear
nor seen with the eye
a silent and solitary prayer.

No stranger present
a communion of all
branches to a butterfly's wing
inside flower and seed hidden
another forest awaits
with a choir of birds to sing.

Communion

Branches leaping
into the billowing wind
dancing amid the morning dew
where sparkles of sun
greet the emerging sky
under a palette
of cloud and blue.

Let seed strike the earth
every heart take flight
beyond our measure of mind
from dappled light to shadow
a communion of elements
even an ocean spray
conscious and alive.

With all my strength surrender
as thunderous waves
assault these shores
only blood and fire mine
until a lasting breath subsides
moments to eternity
the same and more.

Stillness

In stillness of being
behind silent breath
worlds from fire born
enduring countless seasons
time across the intangible
crouching to towering forms.

Surrounded in stretch
of endless forest and field
frozen between ebb and flow
yielding slower than seed
this sediment of light
in stillness I am stone.

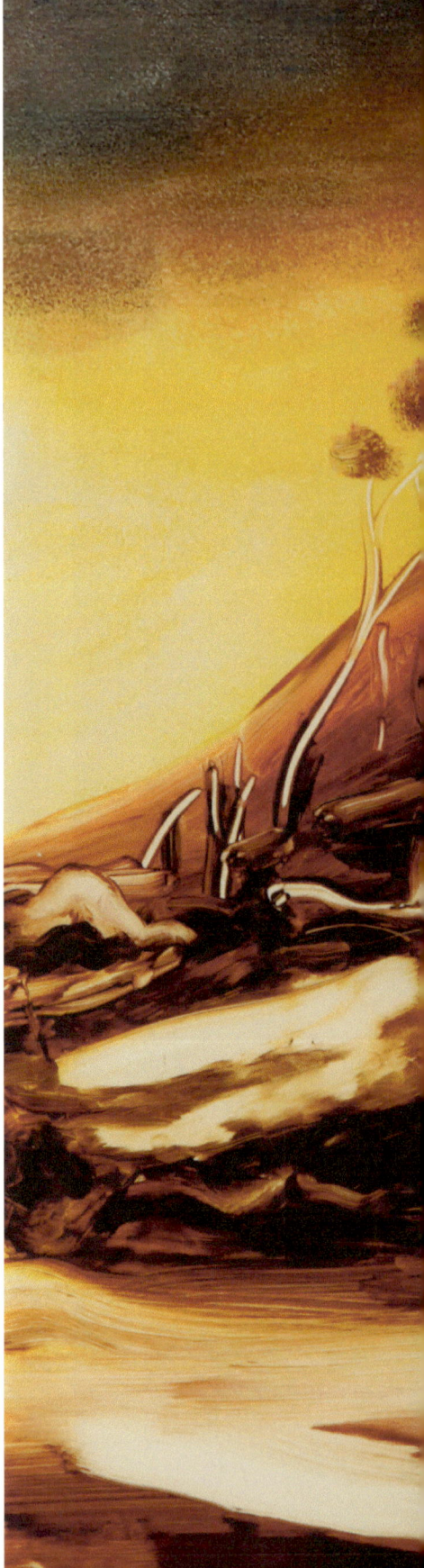

Every World Akin

With the sun rising
inside my heart
the wind billowing
against my skin
where skies of blue
flood these horizons
and a morning light
finds every world akin.

I stretch my eyes
across cloud and distance
my fingers beyond
sense of touch alone
this hour calling
between moments
until a bird's silent wing
sparks a longing for home.

Reflections

Flower unfolding
rising softly
weave come petal of light
cloudless moments
worlds behold
where endless reflections born.

Closer unveiling
awakening now
horizons upon every blossom
hearts promised
to shine eternity
formless moments
brimming worlds beyond
where timeless reflections born.

Night

The night
will have its song
a million smallest fires
lighting our skies long
silent and not one the same.

Like seeds scattered
across oceans vast
dreaming of my return
to become another jewel cast
within this vaulted crown.

Where flight
needs no wing
and the universe all
beneath my own skin
the song will have its night.

Upon a Butterfly's Dream

Upon a butterfly's dream
rising against the storm
never a wavering wing
or fluster of colour
as waters breathe quiet
under rage of air
beckoned to its journey
where new worlds discovered.

By witness of sun
and countless stars
greeting every dawn
and darkest sky
upon a butterfly's courage
rising against the storm
the promise from pupa
awakening to the prize.

Shores to Seasons

Leaves shivering
glistening under an autumn sky
every tree bowed by wind and sun
how swift these gulls glide
circling the air as many wings fold into one.

With masts raised sentinel
tottering upon the horizon
vessels frenzied in a billow of sails
where tides race in a timeless march
let shores to seasons never pale.

Inside Every Heart

If we could touch the sky
let innocence dance
across our days
beyond these horizons
with stars in our reach
and no clouds gathered grey.

Ignite the fire
inside every heart
awaken from this slumber
calm fills the air
when all life hallowed
new worlds waiting in wonder.

The call of oceans
rising in our blood
to another time and tide
with the tempest behind us
hearing its bellow no more
the voyage for none denied.

Across Winter Skies

With sparkle
of morning sun
dapple of cloud
across winter skies
to breathe as a bird
immersed in light
lifted upon wing
when imagination flies.

Trees soaring golden
all flowers aflame
not a moment escaping
these captive eyes
where calm of air
calls to silence
weaving another day
across winter skies.

Sentinel

Forests standing sentinel
like wounded soldiers
scarred to broken
from heart and bough
awaiting some return
and breath of scented green.

Our world dispensed
with hallowed ground
even the sunlight
walled and mortared into place
where shadows of grey prevail.
Nature has become the fringe dweller
within her own domain
all that is artificial serves the world now.
Where could forests take shelter?
Behind our concrete expanse
and towers of commerce?

Yet they will have their time again
as civilisations always rise and fall
weaker than the triumphant seed.

Peregian Beach

Between clamour and calm
every flow and ebb
waves leaping to the shore
where ocean meets horizon
eyes across an endless blue
stretching to seasons more.

Other realms to glimpse
from these lingering clouds
silent above such depths
with gulls pacing sand
and footprints to follow
rhythm behind all in timeless breath.

The Spark

The spark that illuminates the sun
ignites every fire and flame
in silence it dreams to beckon us
to enter its heart and domain.

A compulsion from our light within
never to be quelled
the thread behind our human form
and mind that steers each cell.

No measure could contain
this drop that carries oceans
songs no choir could embrace
one breath to set all in motion.

Driving seed to greater ascent
the force anchoring flesh and flower
a journey beyond and unto itself
dancing across shapeless hours.

Holding us to our given path
through worlds before this world began
in silence it dreams to beckon us
to enter its heart and domain.

I am Flower

I am flower
seeking the dawning sun
my fragrance awakening memories
closer than the hour
lifting senses into unseen horizons.

I am hues green to golden
of light still unfamiliar to the eye
petals fired into form
calling upon leaf and field
a song urgent yet silent
through the passage of seasons.

How I delight in the drenching rain
dance with the swirling wind
even to the rage of storm I stand.
I am no less like you
finding one heart the same
beckoned from seed to bloom.

I draw courage from the earth
my being from all creation
the oceans whispering inside me
where thunder is calmed
and atoms to stars rest in my flame.
I have endured endless summers
the icy clutches of winter
I have seen your civilisations fall to rise again.

Let my voice be heard
let my expression in your world
echo your true origins and knowing
that you may once again return
upon wings of prayer or dreams
behold the garden that has already
long seeded and blossomed deep within you.

Take solace in my beauty
for you are born of soul
and I am flower
seeking the setting sun.

Beyond the Eye

Sea and sky
meeting on the horizon
calm of distant cloud
under autumn light
with air stone silent
where only waves resound.

Sand and sun
across swelling dunes
near one the same
from stretch of land
to beyond the eye
entwine and interplay.

Mooloolaba Summer

Skies of vaulted blue
traversing oceans aflame
waves roaring against the silence
where waters swell
surrender to the shore
then stretch to dawns
and farthest horizons.

Skin and sun glistens
weaving a summer's light
sands ever sparse to the eye
here in a race
for some dappled shade
the clamour of children
and endless play resides.

Concrete and glass
towering in the distance
as sails of white billow and fade
while flags fly unison
under a gathering cloud
gulls hover for a morsel
wings and their shadows pervade.

Walls to castles
built before the hour
upon a whim and another kingdom falls
beyond tides temporal
one glimpse of eternity
come worlds awakened
when every heart is called.

Point Pure

Weaving forest
to mountains resplendent
unearthing distant voices
come the Dreamtime
here and beyond.

From first light born
to landscapes in stone
where ancestors gathered
womb of sacred ways
and all we walk upon.

The Unseen

Flowers spiral on silken threads
woven to stars aeons away
some far distant geometry
extending life to every leaf
trunks in such forests
of colliding formations.

How they dance in waves
moments that pass and interplay
then continue into infinity
such delight to behold
these spheres of intention
fused with force every one.

This surge of tides marching
through the unseen
skies containing only
a fraction of the firmament
our earth a mere point
within universes and how many
one could never imagine.

Each inhalation draws worlds
into our physicality countless again.

Song for the Earth

This is my song for the earth
for every forest and tree
fields in a dance of flowers
stretching shores to wildest seas.

For your sanctuary and surrender
upon another season and tide
to breathe your air becoming
finding solace in a dawning sky.

For every sentient creature
from chrysalis to bird on wing
each birth of fire rising beyond
into the heart of a lasting spring.

For your worlds of endless wonder
my silence and clarion call
this is my song for the earth
new horizons awakening for all.

All Elements Convene

Such a furious wind
as I watch the waves rise
in a relentless march to shore
the open sky pale compared
to the depths of the seas
sunlight gazing behind
a weave of clouds.

Amidst the many sounds
a call can be heard
beneath the rush of moments
a fall into silence
either through eye
knowing or both
an invitation for heart
faint yet familiar
for those that can listen beyond.

Walking across the infinite cosmos
of sand, shells and debris
I look to the horizons and within
where all elements convene.

We Are the Song

We are the song
waiting to be sung
the many coming into one
we are the sleeping
before the awakened heart
the ocean and shores
all of us a part.

We are light
that sparks the sun
works of fire
after the flame is done
we are the forest
in every leaf's design
forged of nature
by no walls confined.

We are worlds
brimming with hopes and dreams
flowers bursting from the eternal seed
we are the thorns
to roses in bloom
each woven from a timeless womb.

We are immeasurable
in all worlds to come
we are the song waiting to be sung.

One Seed

One seed
in darkness waiting
dormant until
a sudden burst of fire
an invisible intent
from some intangible desire
rising and reaching blind
beyond its hidden domain
towards a light unknown.

Under blistering sun
and torrent of rain
breathing through trunk to branch
until flower and fruit
with all its labour
forever fearless to the root
spanning forest to field
returning to the earth again
as another seed awakens.

Breathe the Silence

Let me breathe the silence
here and beyond these walls
to unveil each moment
becoming breath itself.

Not of air nor lung
instead something no words can touch
no eyes can disguise
like fragrance dreaming a flower
as an invitation
where all surrenders upon wings unseen
any thoughts falling from sound
until the silence breathes me.

Poised

We are poised now
for something far greater
dreams that traverse the galaxies
immensities that science
could never fathom nor measure.

Our earth only a miniscule spark
of this wondrous and unseen fire
stirring atom to star alike
the impulse behind our breath and blood.

As every ocean finds its shore
buds wait silent for their burst and bloom
new horizons beckon us upon a ceaseless journey.

We are poised now for something far greater!

The Poet

This is Gerard Traub's first collection of poetry composed to inspire the reader to seek and awaken a deeper connection with nature in all its diversity and splendour. He is also the author of a children's book entitled *Lily the Lotus*. Gerard resides on the Sunshine Coast, Queensland with his family.

The Artist

Nelus Oana was born in Romania and now resides in Australia with his wife in Melbourne. He has exhibited his paintings here and overseas, depicting the beauty and essence of Australia's unique landscape.

www.ingramcontent.com/pod-product-compliance
Lightning Source LLC
Chambersburg PA
CBHW041427010526
44107CB00045B/1528